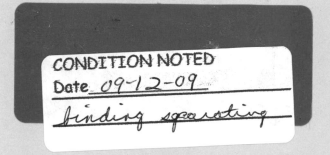

CONDITION NOTED
Date 09-12-09
binding separating

Robin at Hickory Street

SMITHSONIAN'S BACKYARD

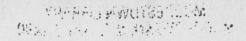
To Chris
— D.M.R.

To KJ
— J.S.

Copyright © 1995 Trudy Management Corporation, 165 Water Street, Norwalk, CT 06856, and the Smithsonian Institution, Washington, DC 20560.

Soundprints is a division of Trudy Management Corporation, Norwalk, Connecticut.

Book Design: Shields & Partners, Westport, CT

First Edition
10 9 8 7 6 5 4 3 2 1
Printed in Singapore

Acknowledgements:
   Our very special thanks to Dr. Gary R. Graves of the Department of Vertebrate Zoology at the Smithsonian's National Museum of Natural History for his curatorial review.

Library of Congress Cataloging-in-Publication Data

Rau, Dana Meachen.

Robin at Hickory Street / by Dana Meachen Rau ; illustrated by Joel Snyder.
        p.   cm.
Summary: While searching for a new home where he can begin a family, Robin often hears "no vacancy" and "no trespassing" chirped at him.
        ISBN 1-56899-168-1
1. Robins — Juvenile fiction. [1. Robins — Fiction. 2. Birds — Fiction. 3. Spring — Fiction.]
I. Snyder, Joel, ill. II. Title.
        PZ10.3.R185Ro 1995   95-6778
        [E] — dc20   CIP
                                                          AC

Robin at Hickory Street

by Dana Meachen Rau
Illustrated by Joel Snyder

Soundprints
Where Children Discover Nature

Winter's song fills the backyard of the bluestone house on Hickory Street. A honeysuckle branch taps a beat on the kitchen window. Wind whistles through swaying spruces. Rhythmic drips of melting ice dot the snow.

Soon this chorus will be replaced by spring's — the sweet murmur of honeybees, the rustling of chipmunks behind the shed and the cheerful melody of a robin who will call this yard his own.

Deep in a southern wooded swampland, Robin has spent the winter. There, he and other robins shared the shelter of the blackgum trees and the water of a nearby stream. Now the longer, warmer days urge them to return north, where Robin was born one year ago.

The birds take to the sky in a blur of gray and red. With a flap of his wings, Robin joins them. The race north has begun. Each robin must look for his own summer home.

The flock of young birds flies by day and roosts at night. Spring wakes tasty worms and delicious grubs for them to eat along the way. The sun and warm rains turn the brown yards to green. Daffodils trumpet the coming of the season.

Over the northern green yards, it is time for the flock to separate. Beneath him, Robin hears older robins who have already arrived, singing, *"cheerily, cheer-up, cheerio!"* But their message is not meant to welcome him. They have found their homes. Robin must search for his elsewhere.

He swoops down to the birdbath of an inviting lawn.

A flicker chitters, and a starling whistles. No robins join the chorus. He ventures onto the grass and struts across the yard.

Taking a deep breath, Robin sings, *"cheerily, cheer-up, cheerio!"*

Like an echo, someone repeats his call!

As Robin turns, he sees the flash of an older robin's fluffed red breast. He dive-bombs toward Robin from a nearby tree. The two birds slam together in a tangle of beaks and feathers. Beating their wings, they separate, fly upward and crash again in midair.

They tumble to the ground. The older bird holds his tail high, tosses back his head and chirps a sharp warning — this yard is already taken.

Robin leaves to find a friendlier home.

Robin glides over yard after yard, stealing a berry here and a beetle there. He tries to get a good night's rest in the branches of a spruce. But by dawn, Robin hears the same tune he has heard everywhere he goes — no vacancy and no trespassing!

Flying low over a dew-spotted lawn, Robin craves his favorite meal — earthworms! He sets down in the backyard of the bluestone house on Hickory Street, watching carefully for attackers. The yard looks clear.

Under his feet in the soft dirt, something squirms. He stops and cocks his head. He catches the glint of a worm just under the soil. His sharp beak stabs the ground and snatches the tip of the pink creature.

The worm stretches like a rubber band, then snaps back to its hole. Poking again, Robin grips it tightly. With one quick jerk, he wins the tug-of-war!

He rubs the stunned worm through the grass so it is less slippery. Then he gulps it down whole.

Another robin lands in the yard. He hops closer, then stops. Robin waits.

Taunting each other, neither will make the first move.

Robin exclaims, *"cheerily, cheer-up, cheerio!"*

Slowly, the stranger backs up.

Robin stands taller and sings again. The other robin flees in fear.
"Cheerio!!" Robin announces at his loudest. There is no answer.
At last, Robin has found his new home!

He flits to a cherry tree that, in summer, will burst with tasty fruit. He hops across the moist ground full of worms. He lands on the windowsill of a small tool shed, a perfect spot for a nest.

Before long, another robin perches on the cherry tree. But her feathers are not as bright as Robin's. He knows not to chase her away. Singing his cheery tune, he invites her to the grass. She flies down to join him. Together they will start a family.

They collect grasses and mud
and make a solid nest, tucked in the
corner of the windowsill.

When it is finished, Robin's
mate lays four blue eggs. For two
weeks, until the chicks are born, she
will keep the eggs warm under her body.
Standing guard, Robin will protect them.
If a squirrel tries to steal the eggs, he will
fight it away with a diving attack.

Behind the bluestone house on Hickory Street, spring is in full swing. Honeybees buzz, chipmunks rustle, and the growing grass sways. Sunlight dances through the open leaves that will give shade to Robin's nest as the season grows warmer.

Robin looks at his yard from the top of a spruce tree. He bursts out with his call to tell strangers beware — this is Robin's yard!

About the Robin

Robins are one of North America's most recognizable birds, found from coast to coast. They adapt well to man-made surroundings such as farms, towns and gardens, and feed on earthworms, insects and many kinds of fruit.

Each spring, robins migrate north from their milder winter grounds. Older robins arrive first and claim yards they may have held the year before. Younger robins arrive later and must find homes wherever they can. All male robins fight each other for remaining territories. The winner of a territory, which is about a half an acre or more in size, then sings loudly to drive away other males. Using a similar song, he attracts a female robin.

When a male and female robin start a family, the female lays three to five bright blue eggs. Once they hatch, the parents spend their days gathering food nearby for their hungry babies. A robin nestling may eat up to 14 feet of earthworms per day!

Glossary

blackgum tree: A tree found near swamplands in the eastern United States.

flicker: A brightly marked woodpecker, common throughout North America.

flock: A group of birds living, feeding or flying together.

grubs: The soft worm-like larval stage of an insect.

honeysuckle: A fragrant shrub with bright flowers rich in nectar.

roost: To settle down for rest or sleep.

starling: A very active bird with a short tail, sharp bill and dark brown or black feathers.

swampland: Wet spongy forested land largely covered by shallow still water.

Points of Interest in this Book

pp. 6-7   river otter, bull frog.

pp. 8-9   daffodils, ladybird beetle.

pp. 8-9, 24-25, 28-29   crocuses.

pp. 12-13   flicker (brown bird), starling (black bird).

pp. 28-29   gray squirrel.